15 ESSENTIAL TIPS FOR YOUR VENDING SIDE-HUSTLE

Vicki May Thorne

Nutrabot, LLC

Vicki May Thorne/Nutrabot, LLC

5303 E 27th Street

Tulsa, OK/ 74114

Ordering Information:

Quantity sales. Special discounts are available on quantity purchases by corporations, associations, and others. For details, contact the "Special Sales Department" at the address above.

15 Essential Tips for your Vending Side Hustle/ Vicki May Thorne. —1st ed.

ISBN 978-1-7362283-0-2

CONTENTS

15 Essential Tips for your Vending Side-Hustle

To my boys: this is how you turn lemons to lemonade! Finish strong.

To my executive coach, Rebecca Gebhart: appreciate all your support, encouragement and agreeing that it's "just like me to sell my business in a pandemic!"

To my folks: thanks for your unwavering encouragement and wise advice to 'break up the set.'

Foreword

At first glance, vending is a simple business: stock a vending machine with soda and chips, refill as needed, collect cash, repeat. We've all bought a cold soda before a flight or class, or a granola bar in a hospital waiting room, and complained about the prices and thought, man, these people are making bank! Personal experiences with vending make it seem accessible and easy. And as far as truly passive income goes, it's a good one for making money while you are working/living/ being elsewhere.

But vending is more complicated and expensive than one expects. There's state and local taxes, insurance, profit margins and foot traffic metrics to consider and many people just don't pay attention to the details when they first get started with a vending business. In this tiny book, I'm sharing my best tips for making more (and keeping more) more money in your vending business, no matter if you own a few machines, a whole route or you are just dreaming of the vending life.

I owned and operated my own full-line vending route for more than four years (from 2016-2020), increased my sales each year, and then successfully sold my business in the middle of the 2020 COVID-19 Pandemic.

"Full-line vending" is the term used for vending that offers drinks and snacks, usually in a combination machine. This is different from candy or toy machine vending, and are taxed differently.

As I close this chapter in my life, I'm writing this book to pass on what I learned and hopefully save you some time, energy and frustration as you grow your own vending business! The tips in the following pages are placed 'in order of emphasis', meaning I'm putting the most important stuff right up front. I try to keep my explanations for each tip brief and to the point.

If you have a burning question about pricing or commissions or the like, feel free to flip straight to the Frequently Asked Questions section!

15 Essential Tips for your Vending Side-Hustle

TIP #1

Stock What People Will Buy

When I started my vending business in early 2016, it was with a healthy vending franchise. The plan was to offer healthy snack options in my machines so that people could have an alternative to sugary soda and greasy chips. I would stock sparkling waters, like La Croix or San Pellegrino, instead of Diet Coke. I would offer energy bars or mixed nuts instead of candy bars. Problem was, people wanted what was familiar to them: brand name drinks and snacks, things that they recognized. I did a great job offering a variety of flavors of, but no one bought them, even though I personally liked them a lot! The same goes for snacks: one fall, I ran across some 'Pumpkin Spice" flavored granola bars and decided to buy several boxes. I thought they would be popular at office buildings--but I ended up with at least 2 boxes of expired products.

When my franchisor declared bankruptcy in 2018, I decided I was free to stock whatever I wanted. I added in popular products like Coke and Doritos and saw a quick increase in sales.

Each location will like certain products, but by offering what is generally popular (and full of sugar), your sales will be stronger. If you have the ability to track your sales by location, you will be able to tell what products are the most popular at each location. Try to stock the same items in the majority of your machines, even if you have to reduce or adjust the number of products in accordance with how fast things tend to sell.

T I P # 2

Sign A Contract When Placing Machines

There is nothing more exciting than placing a machine at a new location. All that foot traffic! All those hungry, thirsty people! All those sales! Before you install the machine, however, I would strongly recommend that you sign a contract with your location that puts in writing what you agree to do in terms of servicing, stocking, and maintenance. A contract should also spell out how long your partnership is anticipated to last. I put my contract length as a year (12 months), renewable by mutual agreement.

Finally, your contract needs to put in writing whether or not you are paying a commission and how often it's to be paid.

A contract does not have to be written by a lawyer. You can write your own and customize it for each situation. When I first started in vending, I did not use a contract with my first few placements, and it cost me one of my best office building locations. This office high-rise had a vending room on the ground floor with several competing machines, including mine. After two years of strong sales (but no paid commission), the owners of the building signed an exclusivity agreement with a regional vending brand. I had to relocate my machine with very little notice and zero recourse. Similarly, if the location is a dud and you want to move your machine, you'll need to give notice in accordance with your contract. I put in my contract (after another bad experience--this time with a bar) that if the machine needs to be removed before six months have passed, the location needs to pay for the removal. This cut way down on "let's try it and see" locations. Paying to move the machines around is a cost that can really add up; it's best to seek long-term placements and thoroughly vet your potential locations before you install your machine.

(Check out my website: victoriamthorne.com for a sample contract & location vetting survey!)

TIP #3

Inventory your Stock Regularly and Precisely

Taking inventory is not anyone's idea of a fun time, but since your profit relies on how many tiny sales you make in a week, you need to know how many bags of chips and cans of Coke you have both on hand and in your machines. It doesn't matter if you use inventory software or just a spreadsheet, but you need to take inventory every time you service a machine. Additionally, you must have a count for your excess inventory, so that you know what you need to purchase to fill your machines. Most of your inventory should be stocked in your machines, not sitting in storage. Spend as little as you can on inventory and manage it well; don't be afraid to move inventory between machines if some items sell better at one location over another.

Your inventory costs should be as low as possible. Shop sales, buy wholesale if you can, and know your per item cost. Knowing how much you paid for something will help you mark up accordingly. There's a big difference between paying 18 cents for Doritos and 50 cents for a specialty chip. If you do stock something special, place it in a prominent spot, price it well (but don't try to gouge), and spread out your inventory. If you try a new product, put a limited amount in a few machines and see how it goes. If you sell out, restock! If you don't sell through all of the stock in 3 to 4 weeks, don't bother restocking.

TIP #4

Track and Minimize Your Expenses

Expenses related to vending can include buying stock, mileage for driving to service machines, memberships to wholesale clubs, and supplies for cleaning and maintenance. Keep your expenses low and keep track of them. The primary reason for tracking expenses is that it helps a great deal at tax time. Because you are running your own business, many of the expenses associated with operating your business are tax deductible.* The single largest deduction is mileage, so track your miles as you drive to pick up stock, do routine stocking, and reach out to new locations.

You can use a simple spreadsheet, but there are a number of good apps for tracking mileage and even apps for capturing receipts for accounting software (Quickbooks, Wave, etc). Whatever method you choose, DO attend to your expenses regularly. I would recommend weekly or monthly. Then, when tax time rolls around, you won't have to try to compile a year's worth of expenses at one time.

I am not a tax professional. Please check with a CPA to find out more about tax deductible items.

TIP #5

Prioritize Your Taxes

In order to run a legal business, you should consult your state's tax department and see what kind of paperwork you need to complete. In my state, I needed a business permit, and I filed for an LLC. In addition, you should expect to pay state sales tax on goods sold. In my state, vending qualified for a sales tax waiver on goods bought (to stock my machines), but then I had to pay the sales tax on goods sold at a later date.

Additionally, your state or city may require you to purchase a decal to adhere to your machine to show that you are in compliance. Costs vary, but these sorts of decals are usually good for an entire year. In my state, the tax decals for coin-operated vending over 25 cents (i.e. most snack/drink vending) cost $75/per machine.

Taxes certainly are no fun to pay, but what's worse is having to pay additional fees when you get caught without the proper decals or permits. One year, I delayed buying and installing my tax decals until about six months after the deadline, and the delay cost me. I thought no one was checking on the tax decals on vending machines, but I was wrong! The code enforcement person put bright red stickers all over the out-of-compliance machine, including over all of the card, bill, and coin receptors, literally blocking sales.

Not only was it embarrassing, but in order to restore the functionality of the machine, I also had to pay an additional $100 fine to the state tax commission.

Make it a **priority** to pay your taxes, buy your vending decals, and stay on top of the tax requirements. Neglecting these things will cost you more money and add lots of paperwork and headaches to your life!

TIP #6

Save the Snacks for Customers

There's nothing better than an ice cold drink after a hot afternoon of stocking vending machines. Unfortunately, if you eat or drink your own stock, you are hurting your business in two ways: First, you are reducing the number of possible sales by not having those items in your machines. Second, for tax purposes, you will have to account for stock that is not sold. Yes, the sales tax worksheets will specifically ask how much product you consumed!

Early in my vending career, I would regularly help myself to snacks and drinks as I serviced my machines. Eventually, I noticed that it added up over the weeks and months and losing the potential profit wasn't worth it to me. However, expired goods are fair game, so stick to snacking from the out-of-dates, which brings us to Tip #7.

TIP #7

Watch Your Expiration Dates

Snacks and drinks have wildly variable
expiration dates. Some snacks are fresh and
still taste good for long periods of time,
while others may only be good for a few
weeks. Depending on what you are stocking
in your machines, you may need to watch
the expiration dates of your items, and be
prepared to reduce your price in order to
sell them in a timely manner. If a whole row
of snacks goes out of date because no one

is buying them, then you've lost the money that you paid to purchase the product. Customers will absolutely notice if items are out of date and stale, and they will complain. Then you have to issue a refund, which is a major inconvenience.

Maybe you've heard the phrase "First In, First Out"? What this means is that when you buy new stock, put it behind stock that's already in the machine. The stock that you put in first should stay at the front so that it can be purchased. A less obvious hack is to only put in as much stock as will sell in a reasonable amount of time--you don't have to fill the coil all the way to the top. If it's a new product and you aren't sure how it's going to sell, just put in six to eight to see how they do.

TIP #8

Double Up on Popular Items

If you notice that something is selling particularly well, put in another row of it! There's no vending rule that says you have to have a unique item in every single coil, and you will likely have more sales if you double up on popular items. I had a location that was wild for Veggie Straw chips. They were always sold out when I went to restock, so I added another row of Veggie Straws right next to the first one. Sales increased, and I was able to utilize my stock more effectively.

Another benefit of having two (or even three) rows of a popular product is that it can help you manage your time a bit better. Fewer products to stock means that you'll be able to do inventory and refill that much more quickly.

TIP #9

Donate Your Expired Goods

If you ever find yourself with snacks or drinks that are expired and out of date, you can definitely eat them yourself...or you can turn a waste of money into a tax deduction by donating them to a nonprofit. Now, I wouldn't recommend you donate them to a food bank (most don't take expired food items), but if there's an organization that serves folks with food needs, your expired snacks may be welcome. For example, I donate my expired snacks to a local organization that provides transportation assistance and bikes to people experiencing homelessness. While the organization doesn't distribute food as part of its programs, the people that they serve are always happy to pick up some extra snacks when they come in for transportation assistance.

TIP #10

Build a Relationship with Location Staff

The main customers that you will have at any vending location are the employees of that location. Even if the location has a lot of outside foot traffic, the people that are there the most (and who are often hungry and bored) are the employees. They are the ones who will interact the most with your machine (as customers) and your machine's other customers. They are the ones who will hear the good, bad, and ugly from your customers. They are a great source of information and input. Learn their names and their favorite snack items. They can be allies as you learn the location and clientele. If you have extra or expired snacks, giving them a free product will make them happy and make them glad to see you when you stop by to stock.

TIP #11

Grow Through Referrals

When it's time to grow your business and add a new machine to your route, ask for referrals from the contacts that you have at your current locations, like employees and building managers. You can ask if they have other buildings that they manage, or if they know of any other businesses like theirs that might be interested in your machines, etc.

One of my first locations was an after school music program that served a wide variety of families from across the city. One of the parents that attended was also an administrator at a local magnet school. When she asked the music program's staff about the vending machine, they were able to put her in touch with me. As a result, I was able to install a vending machine at the school which had over 400 students and more than 30 staff.

When you go to meet with and vet a potential location, take the person you are meeting with a few items, like a drink and snack. If you ask about their favorite snacks in advance of this meeting, you can take those; if not, just take your best sellers or a product you want to highlight. This functions as a professional gesture and a thank you, as well as a reminder after you leave of how nice it would be to have snacks on-site in the form of a vending machine!

(Check out my website, victoriamthorne.com do download a sample referral form!)

TIP #12

Be a Professional

While you don't need to have a custom wrapped vehicle or branded uniforms, you can be a professional on your vending route by having appropriate tools needed to do the job. Things like a cart or trolley to load in stock are essential as it saves your back and saves time spent making multiple trips to bring in stock. You might also consider carrying a small set of tools to help you solve problems on the go. For example, a screwdriver can attend to loose screws and unjam a coin slot. Lastly, it's a good idea to carry business cards with your business-specific contact information. Both a separate phone number (try using Google Voice or Sideline) and a dedicated business email are important because they provide a secure, professional way for business contacts to reach you. For example, if a building manager has a potential referral to pass on to you, they will be more likely to email you at BizName@email.com rather than FirstName420@email.com.

A word about custom shirts/branded apparel: I did spend some money on a few branded clothes items early in my career. I bought four sporty, colorful shirts in my brand colors (blue and orange, plus black and gray) at JCPenny then paid a friend to apply my slogan and logo on them. I also had my logo put onto my work coat and a few aprons. All of that cost about $100, including clothing costs. I wore those shirts whenever I went to stock machines, to shop for stock, to meet potential locations, and to deliver commission checks. Basically, whenever I was acting on behalf of my business, I wore my apparel. It helped me to feel and look more professional and "put together." When I hired a stocking assistant, they were also provided with a logoed shirt, as I wanted them to be easily identifiable as part of my team. Ultimately, you could spend money on fancy cards or custom apparel, but you don't really need to in order to do your job professionally. Focus on providing regular machine service and paying out commissions when you've said you are going to pay them.

TIP #13

Hire Carefully

There is great value in doing the work of vending yourself; inventory, re-stock, and cash collection should take an hour per machine or less . There are many vending operators who service their routes in addition to other job(s) and like that they are able to do so with some flexibility. As your route grows, it may become necessary to hire someone to help you with the weekly tasks.

Be very careful about who you hire because when an additional person has keys to your machine, you increase the chances that your stock and your cash collections could be tampered with. The person you hire must have very clear guidelines on how they are to do the service tasks and how long that should take (if you are paying them by the hour) and how the cash collected is to be handled. Are they depositing every week? Or after every service? Or are they just returning the cash to you, and you handle the deposit? Do you want to do cash collection yourself? How do you want the coins handled? Most importantly, they need to be aware that you are monitoring their cash handling and that you are tracking the sales and know how much to expect in each machine.

Before you hire someone as a stocking assistant, decide how much you can afford to pay, then compare your rate with what other vending companies are paying to make sure it's comparable. Think through how often they will receive raises, what kind of bonuses you might offer them for referrals, etc. Adding someone to your vending team means that you are growing! However, payroll can be a significant expense, so think carefully about paying someone else to do the work of stocking and servicing your machines.

TIP #14

Pay Attention to Pricing

A major gripe about vending machines is that the snacks and drinks inside are overpriced. What I found to be true was that items that are overpriced simply do not sell. I learned to adjust my pricing as needed. When I started, I aimed for at least a dollar profit on each item. For example, a bag of Doritos costs me 18 cents each, so I started out pricing them at $1.25. In some locations, this price was fine and they sold well, like if there were no other snack options around. In other locations, if there were competing machines or other food options within walking distance, they sold better at $1.00. Don't be afraid to reduce prices if items aren't selling. It's better to make a few cents less profit than make fewer sales and have stock that goes out of date.

Something else to consider is your pricing for credit card sales vs. cash sales. I, personally, am a big fan of offering credit cards as a payment option, primarily because fewer people carry cash than they used to. Of course, having a credit card option means that there are additional costs that come with it- you may have to buy a card reader and install it (costs vary, but $200-400 is typical), or there may be a monthly fee in addition to a transaction fee. Transaction fees can vary from 3% to 6%. In order to offset this cost, some vending operators will charge a different price for credit sales: maybe a bag of chips costs $1.35 instead of $1.25 for a cash purchase. Any time you see a sign on a vending machine saying that it offers a "cash discount," it means you are paying more if you use your card.

TIP #15

Customize! But Skip Special Requests

As I mentioned, about halfway through my four year vending journey, I switched from a "healthy" snacks only model to more of a "custom" vending model. In addition to the sports drinks and sparkling waters I had been stocking, I started stocking popular soda brands, iced teas, and even energy drinks. I emphasized that I was able to customize what was offered in each machine as unique to the location. I kept the healthy items that sold well and offered in-demand items as well. I even asked the folks at my locations for product suggestions, which people are always happy to give. At a location with a lot of outdoor construction, we stocked plenty of water, but got numerous requests for Monster energy drinks. My rule of thumb was that if I got the same request from multiple people, I went ahead and stocked some.   I would warn you to stay away from overly specific requests, however. For example, at one of my locations, the property manager I was working with requested some of those mini, disposable toothbrushes. I stocked them for her, alongside my standard snacks and drinks, but it took more than six months to sell through just one box!

Frequently Asked Questions

Reminder: these are all my personal opinion and I am speaking from my experience only; you are always welcome to run your business any way you see fit.

How do I set my prices?

There are a few things to consider when you are setting prices: First, you should always be able to cover what you paid, and you should know your price per item. To calculate your price per item, simply divide the cost (price you paid for the product, pre-tax) by the number of units purchased.

So, if a box of Flamin Hot Cheetos (a consistent top seller for me) is $13.98 at Sam's this week and there are 50 in the box, then they cost me 28 cents, per bag. Knowing that, I can then set my minimum price at 50 cents; that's the lowest I should ever reduce to. A nice round $1.00 is a super fair price, $1.25 is a sweet spot, and $1.50 might work for high demand locations. I'm not a fan of pricing gouging and I've learned that it doesn't really work. If your prices are too high, people simply won't buy. Then you run the risk of your product going out of date, and you losing the "investment" in your product.

Do I Have to Pay a Commission?

Whether or not you offer a commission is completely up to you. I found it to be a nice bargaining chip to use when lining up placements, but I also found that they are typically not worth the hassle. I paid out my commissions quarterly, so as to save myself a monthly task, and only paid 10% on profits. Doing commission checks was time consuming and while the amounts were relatively small to the organizations ($20-$80), it added up quickly on my end. Then add in the additional time spent calculating the commissions, writing and sending checks, which incur additional expenses for postage or eCheck software. I'd certainly do it differently. Some vending folks don't offer commission at all, and say that if you can't get a placement without a commission then you didn't do a good enough job selling the value of having a vending machine on site. While that can be true, do keep in mind that larger vending businesses likely ARE offering commission and at higher rates than you can match (20-30% is not unheard of). A small commission may help you seal the deal, but just be aware that it's not always worth it.

Where do I buy my stock?

Depending on what kind of items you are stocking, you can buy your stock wherever is most convenient or has the best prices for your area. In my area, we have a number of easily accessible Sam's Clubs and only one Costco. Check into whatever local wholesale club is close to you! I purchased the bulk of my inventory from Sams, but also ordered some specialty products online. A wholesale club may be a good option for convenience, but you may find other options by talking with others in your town or industry. For example, a local vending guy I know hosts a weekly delivery from a national vending supplier that other small vending business owners partake in; they place an order as a group and split the delivery costs. Beware of buying stock from Dollar Stores, they are often very close to or past expiration and will not last long in your machines.

How do I "vet" a potential location?

A location needs to have two things for it to be profitable: people with money and minimal competition. It is your job to ask lots of questions and find out some key information when you are considering a location to place a machine. First, ask about foot traffic: you want at least 50 people passing by your machine every day; you will still make sales with fewer than that, but you'll quickly become dissatisfied with the number of sales and wish for a new location. For example, a school is a great location, **if** there are enough staff and if the students are allowed access to the machine. If a school has a 'no vending for students before 3pm' rule (some do, you have to ask!), then your customers are essentially only the adults on campus (and the occasional parent passing through the lobby), and that's likely not going to meet your foot traffic needs. Secondly, ask

directly about competing food and beverage options: "Where do you guys buy snacks from now?" If there's a gas station within walking distance, don't bother. If there's a cafeteria or a vending "room," be cautious. Competition isn't necessarily a bad thing, customers like options, but do realize you'll just be getting part of the sales that already exist. An outdoor location is a bad idea, unless you have an outdoor-designed model, like commercial grade beverage machines. Don't be surprised if you run up against exclusivity contracts; and be sure to address them in your placement contract.

How do I handle demands for a refund?

You handle it by knowing what your protocol is on refunds, before you ever get a request. And you will have many! I've found that there are two types of refund requests: legitimate and bogus. If you are stocking a machine and someone approaches you with a story about how they lost money to your machine or they didn't get an item they paid for, ask them for more information. If they can offer specifics, have them email you with the request (business cards come in very handy here); if they can get me the specifics, I am usually happy to provide a refund or coupon!

If they are insistent about a refund on the spot, you've likely got a bogus claim on your hands. On the other hand, if I felt the person was genuine, I would offer them the drink or snack they were trying to purchase initially. My personal policy was to decline to give a cash refund. This is largely a safety-minded approach, as busting out your bank bag stuffed with cash, to provide a few dollars refund isn't very smart. Vending machines do miss vends and exact change doesn't always happen, so be understanding, but do have a process for how you address refund claims.

What are some 'good' locations?

Let me run through some of my location experiences and see if you can spot the theme:

Eyelash Salon- NO (too quiet, too small, less than 10 staff)

Church gyms- meh (good traffic, but the healthy snacks didn't sell well)

YMCA- good until a competing machine moved in; sold the hell out of some protein bars.

High-rise office buildings- good, but very competitive

Afterschool- varies, but good if there's a wide mix of ages, especially adults.

Bars/Music Venues- annoying and the reason there's a 'you pay for removal if you break contract at 6 months or less' clause in my placement contract.

Event Center- very good, before COVID

Charter School- check to make sure the students can purchase from the machines; or else you need a staff of 40 minimum.

Multi-use Facility- good! Really good. Strong foot traffic/construction crews- #1 location when I sold my assets in 2020.

Dispensary-good, especially if both staff and customers have access; actually saw a sales increase during COVID.

Spot the theme? Foot traffic!
The more foot traffic the better!

Good luck, ya'll! -VMT

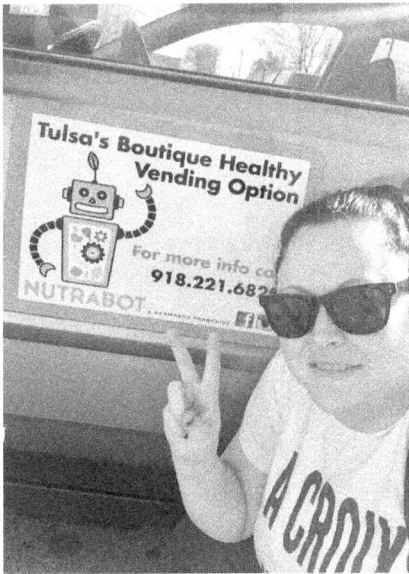

15 Essential Tips for your Vending Side-Hustle

www.ingramcontent.com/pod-product-compliance
Lightning Source LLC
Chambersburg PA
CBHW030535210326
41597CB00014B/1150